To:

_____

From:

_____

Date:

_____

Published by Christian Art Publishers
PO Box 1599, Vereeniging, 1930, RSA

© 2022
First edition 2022

Designed by Christian Art Publishers

Cover designed by Christian Art Publishers

Images used under license from Shutterstock.com

Set in 11 on 14 pt Cronos Pro
by Christian Art Publishers

Printed in China

ISBN 978-1-77637-091-7 (Faux Leather)
ISBN 978-1-77637-116-7 (Hardcover)

22 23 24 25 26 27 28 29 30 31 – 10 9 8 7 6 5 4 3 2 1

DEDICATED
TO MY DAUGHTERS
Emma, Leah, and Anna

101
Prayers
for
Women

JOANNA TEIGEN

CHRISTIAN ART
PUBLISHERS

INTRODUCTION

"There is a voice that says, 'Prove that you are a good person.' Another voice says, 'You'd better be ashamed of yourself.' There also is a voice that says, 'Nobody really cares about you,' and one that says, 'Be sure to become successful, popular, and powerful.' But underneath all these often very noisy voices is a still, small voice that says, 'You are My Beloved, My favor rests on you.' That's the voice we need most of all to hear ... That's what prayer is. It is listening to the voice that calls us 'My Beloved'."

– Henri J. M. Nouwen

As you make these prayers your own, may you know God's love that changes everything.

"Call to Me and I will answer you and tell you great and unsearchable things you do not know."

Jeremiah 33:3

LIVE IN THE LIGHT

Be on your guard; stand firm in the faith;
be courageous; be strong.
Do everything in love.

1 CORINTHIANS 16:13-14

Lord,

You say in the last days that sin will run rampant in this world. Pride, violence, and greed will dominate our culture (2 Timothy 3:1-4). Your beautiful name will be slandered while evil men are praised. The precious children of God will be rejected and abused. Yet in the darkness, Your light shines on.

Please use me, Lord, to "overcome evil with good" (Romans 12:21). Give me compassion to love the weak, the rejected, and the marginalized in my community. When others call me a fool for believing in Jesus, give me courage to share the reason for my hope (1 Peter 3:15). Keep me alert to the enemy's schemes.

Overcome my doubts and fears. Fill me with grace. May I be faithful to You to the end.

Amen.

A CLEAN HEART

*If we confess our sins, He is faithful and just
and will forgive us our sins and purify us
from all unrighteousness.*

1 John 1:9

Lord,

You know the stubborn places in my heart. The resentment I hold against those who hurt me. The pride I feel in the face of others' failures. The broken promises. The determination to have my own way. The destructive words spoken in anger. The gossip and joking at another's expense. The selfishness that chooses to grab instead of share. My sin is wide open for You to see.

Today I ask for a clean heart and mind. Purify me from every sinful desire, word, and action. Renew a right spirit so I can freely love and obey You in everything.

Thank You for never turning away from me. Your forgiveness and love are my life.

Amen.

WATCHING MY WORDS

Set a guard over my mouth, Lord;
keep watch over the door of my lips.

PSALM 141:3

Lord,

A single word of gossip can tear a friendship apart. One little white lie can destroy trust and ruin credibility with others. Arrogant bragging or slander will damage reputations and sabotage success. Like You say, the tongue is a fire with the power to burn one's life to the ground (James 3:6).

I bear the scars of cruel words that left me broken and insecure. Keep me from doing the same harm to my friends and loved ones. Keep every kind of critical, crude, or hateful speech out of my conversations. Purify my heart and fill me with love since "the mouth speaks what the heart is full of" (Matthew 12:34). Use my words to bless and encourage, honor and heal.

I want to praise and worship You most of all.

Amen.

THE POWER OF GOODNESS

*Bless those who persecute you; bless
and do not curse. Do not be overcome
by evil, but overcome evil with good.*

ROMANS 12:14, 21

Lord,

Pressing into Jesus pulls me away from some people in my life. They don't understand my commitment to Your church. My lifestyle and habits leave them confused. If I refuse to join in gossip, slander, or rude humor, I'm pushed to the side. As I humble myself to obey You, I'm told I'm arrogant and self-righteous. I'm paying the price to follow You as I suffer rejection like Jesus.

Fill me with Your love for the lost. Instead of reacting in anger to others' arguments or criticism, keep me gentle and patient. Give strength to follow You and hold on to Your Word no matter the resistance I face. Bear Your Spirit's fruit in me so that goodness and love shine Your light to everyone.

Amen.

MADE FOR A PURPOSE

*For we are God's handiwork, created in Christ
Jesus to do good works, which God
prepared in advance for us to do.*

EPHESIANS 2:10

Lord,

In Your great love, You called me to be Your own. As Your child I am saved from the despair of a life with no meaning. You give me purpose in the good works You prepared for me from the beginning.

Your Spirit equips me with gifts beyond my natural ability so I can serve and love in Your name. I am crafted by Your hand to build Your kingdom and shine Your light in the world.

Thank You for moving me out of the center of my own universe. As my King, take my life and use it to accomplish Your beautiful, perfect plan. Reveal each day's special assignment so I can obey with confidence. Your will is my delight (Psalm 40:8).

Amen.

Don't worry about anything; instead, pray about everything. Tell God what you need, and thank Him for all He has done.

PHILIPPIANS 4:6

YOU KNOW MY NEEDS

*" ... for your Father knows what
you need before you ask Him."*

MATTHEW 6:8

Lord,

You know everything the future holds. No hardship or trouble I face will catch You off guard. Because You're in control of all things, I don't have to fear tomorrow. You stand ready to meet my needs and catch me before I fall.

Thank You for Your loving care. Like an attentive Father, You watch over me every moment. You know when my resources are running low. If I grow tired, afraid, or discouraged, You draw close to build me up. Your Word holds the wisdom I need for whatever comes my way. Perfect love never lets me go.

I pray I walk in bold confidence because You're with me. Teach me to abide in You every moment. Let peace and hope fill my life as I grow more and more sure of Your love.

Amen.

LOVE IS A VERB

*If anyone has material possessions and sees
a brother or sister in need but has no pity
on them, how can the love of God be
in that person? Dear children, let us not
love with words or speech but with
actions and in truth.*

1 JOHN 3:17-18

Lord,

I've been taught to strive for independence. I pretend I'm strong, even when struggling with needs and fears. It's hard to admit defeat and ask for help. And in my self-focus, I fail to recognize the hurts and burdens of those around me.

Overcome my self-sufficiency with Your love. Give me courage to both share my troubles and offer help to others. Open my eyes to see who in my life is lonely, troubled, and overwhelmed by difficulty.

Fill my heart with Jesus' compassion. Put my faith in action so Your love is demonstrated in all I do.

Amen.

FAITH IN THE FIGHT

*"For I am the LORD your God who takes hold
of your right hand and says to you,
Do not fear; I will help you."*

Lord,

I do not feel like a warrior. After fighting for so long, I've been knocked to the ground. My supporters and assets, hard work and creativity have been trampled by the problem I face. Alone and broken, my hope for victory is gone.

Today I admit defeat. "Apart from You, I can do nothing" (John 15:5). Let me know You as my helper in this impossible situation. Lead me by the hand in the way I should go. Rescue me from trouble. Overcome my enemies. Give me courage to stand up and face another day. Use this trial to prove Your power and build my faith in Your love.

May I receive more of You than I've ever known before.

Amen.

ONLY JESUS

"You do not want to leave too, do you?"
Jesus asked the Twelve. Simon Peter
answered him, "Lord, to whom shall we go?
You have the words of eternal life."

JOHN 6:67-68

Lord,

Political leaders promise their policies will fix what's broken in our country. Social media offers a free space to battle my opponents in the name of self-expression. Banks offer generous loans so I can buy a form of happiness. Every romantic movie promises soul satisfaction in the arms of a loved one.

After tasting what the world has to offer, I find no experience, possession, or relationship is able to fill the emptiness in my heart.

Thank You for Jesus. He is "the way and the truth and the life" who made the one and only way to You, Father (John 14:6). Your love eliminates fear and despair. Your great salvation gives eternal life. I am Yours!

Amen.

STRENGTH IN THE SADNESS

Why, my soul, are you downcast?
Why so disturbed within me?

PSALM 43:5

Lord,

I'm overwhelmed and depressed. I feel like one more set-back or disappointment will crush me. My faith is fragile as I wait for You to answer my prayers and bring relief. Looking for help and support, I feel alone and unseen by everyone. Only You can rescue me from this pain.

Rekindle the hope in my heart today. Be my Champion who fights my battles and protects me from harm. "Keep my lamp burning" and turn my darkness into light (Psalm 18:28). Restore my trust in Your power that is greater than any obstacle I face. Let me rest in Your love that has never failed me yet.

By Your Spirit, help me to worship. Put words of praise in my mouth for all You've done. You are life!

Amen.

The LORD hears His people
when they call to Him for help.
He rescues them
from all their troubles.

PSALM 34:17

LEADING IN LOVE

Brothers and sisters, if someone is caught in a sin, you who live by the Spirit should restore that person gently. But watch yourselves, or you also may be tempted.

GALATIANS 6:1

Lord,

Negative attitudes are contagious. Casual conversations lure me into gossip before I realize what I'm saying. Others' excitement to shop and spend stirs greed in my heart. Broken relationships around me feed a critical spirit of my own loved ones.

While You call me to "spur one another on toward love and good deeds" (Hebrews 10:24), I can be tempted to sin instead.

Use me as an example of Your love. Let me influence my friends and family to trust Your Word. Teach me to openly share Your truth. When I encounter dishonesty, selfishness, or pride, give me strength to do what's right. Let my actions match my words as I live out true faith in You.

Amen.

HANDS OF RESCUE

My brothers and sisters, if one of you
should wander from the truth and someone
should bring that person back, remember this:
Whoever turns a sinner from the error
of their way will save them from death
and cover over a multitude of sins.

JAMES 5:19-20

Lord,

My heart is grieved as friends and loved ones are turning from You. They reject the truth of Your Word. They sin without remorse. They separate themselves from the community of Your people. Determined to go their own way, they are blind to the destruction ahead.

Give me courage and wisdom to know what to do. Show me how to speak the truth in love, inviting them to return to You. Make me persistent in prayer, believing You can rescue and give abundant, eternal life in Christ. Fill me with relentless love that longs for their salvation.

Amen.

WAITING FOR YOU

*Hope deferred makes the heart sick,
but a longing fulfilled is a tree of life.*

PROVERBS 13:12

Lord,

You know the most deep and constant longings of my heart. Day after day, I call out to You in prayer and wait for You to answer. As time goes by my hope wears thin. Do You hear me? Will You meet my needs? Do You know the heartache I feel? Will You bring the relief and blessing I'm hoping for?

I need strength to keep trusting and asking. Give me faith to believe You will "bring about justice for [Your] chosen ones, who cry out to [You] day and night" (Luke 18:7). Restore my confidence in Your power and love as I see You working.

Lift my spirits and fill me with overwhelming joy as You open Your hand to satisfy my heart's desires. You are faithful and good.

Amen.

PURE IN HEART

The perverse of heart shall be far from me;
I will have nothing to do with what is evil.

PSALM 101:4

Lord,

With simply the touch of a screen, a flood of images and entertainment open to my view. Celebrities, newscasters, and political figures shout for my ear's attention. I'm confronted by human pride and perversion at every turn.

Show me how to live as a child of light in the darkness of this world (Ephesians 5:8). Teach me to take control of my thoughts so I focus on what is true, lovely, and excellent at all times (Philippians 4:8).

Give me discernment to recognize lies disguised as truth so I stand firm on Your Word. Grow the fruit of self-control in my life – I need strength to walk away from places and people who entice me away from You. I want to please You, Father, in everything.

Amen.

PEACE IN THE NIGHT

When you lie down, you will not be afraid;
when you lie down, your sleep will be sweet.

PROVERBS 3:24

Lord,

Sleepless nights have left me exhausted. I toss and turn, fretting over today's problems and yesterday's regrets. My imagination pictures every kind of disaster that could strike me and the ones I love. Anxiety and fatigue are leaving me irritable, fearful, and sad. If I can't find rest, I'll fall apart.

Tonight, I want to trust You as the Father who loves me. Ease my worries by filling my thoughts with truth and the comfort of Your promises. Give wisdom for my steps so I can walk through life with confidence. Make me faithful to obey You in all things.

Bless me with the sweet peace of a clean conscience. Heal my body and spirit of aching pain. Let me know sweet sleep, Lord.

Amen.

Devote yourselves to prayer
with an alert mind
and a thankful heart.

COLOSSIANS 4:2

OPEN MY EYES

See if there is any offensive way in me,
and lead me in the way everlasting.

PSALM 139:24

Lord,

So often, I'm blind to my own faults. I don't realize my words are hurtful.

I miss opportunities to show kindness or compassion. Wrapped up in my own concerns, I fail to put others first. I forget to pray or keep the promises I've made. In my distraction and self-focus, I sin. I need You to shine Your light in the hidden corners of my heart.

Examine me and reveal which attitudes need mending. Interrupt my habits to teach new patterns of living and loving. Soften my stubborn heart and give me humility to take advice. Make me new so I bear the fruit of Your Spirit. I want to obey without compromise. May I live a life worthy of the calling I've received from You (Ephesians 4:1).

Amen.

PERFECT TIMING

The Lord is not slow in keeping His promise, as some understand slowness. Instead He is patient with you, not wanting anyone to perish, but everyone to come to repentance.

2 PETER 3:9

Lord,

Wherever I look I see suffering. Violence. Terror. Natural disasters. War and political upheaval. Divorce and abuse. Poverty and disease. As this world crumbles around me, it's hard to hold on to hope. You seem slow in coming to save us and make things new.

Help me to see Your love in the waiting. Teach me to trust in Your compassion, for You want each person to turn to Jesus. Put Your desire into my heart to see everyone saved and set free.

Let my days be used to relieve pain, offer hope, and share the good news of the gospel. Thank You for the glory that is to come for all who love You.

Amen.

KNOW LOVE,
NO FEAR

There is no fear in love. But perfect love drives out fear, because fear has to do with punishment. The one who fears is not made perfect in love.

1 JOHN 4:18

Lord,

Before I believed in Jesus, I had much to fear. My sin had separated me from You. I was blind to the truth. I had no defense against Satan and his lies. My future seemed dark and hopeless. Your mercy and love seemed too good to be true.

Thank You for Your constant, unconditional love that set me free from fear. In Christ there is no condemnation. My future is secure – You've written my name on Your hands. Nothing can separate me from Your love. Instead of punishment, You promise glorious, eternal life with You.

I'm accepted, cherished, and kept under Your wing. Your perfect grace gives me peace forever.

Amen.

FULLY SATISFIED

They feast on the abundance of Your house;
You give them drink from Your river of delights.

PSALM 36:8

Lord,

This life leaves me hungry and unsatisfied. I'm lonely for connection. My heart desires peace and rest. In my work, I want to feel purposeful and truly make a difference. Broken relationships cry for reconciliation.

The shame of sin stirs an ache to be made clean and whole. The enemy tempts me with pleasure and material things. Apart from You, my human heart is always wanting more.

Yet more than anything, I want to taste and see that You are good (Psalm 34:8). Show me how to pull up a chair to Your table and feast on Your love, mercy, and truth. Satisfy my thirst with Your living water.

Fill my soul with Your Spirit, my mouth with Your praise, and my mind with Your wisdom. Be my everything.

Amen.

A BROKEN HEART

*Even my close friend, someone
I trusted, one who shared my bread,
has turned against me.*

PSALM 41:9

Lord,

My friend was a sister to my heart. She walked hard roads with me and celebrated life's precious moments by my side. I placed my insecurities, my hopes and dreams, and my deepest struggles in her hands. She was knit into the very fabric of my life.

I feel broken by my friend's betrayal. Her rejection has left me weak and alone. Guarded and hurt, I don't know who to trust. This loss leaves a void that seems impossible to fill.

Help me to know You as my true friend. Comfort me with Your faithful love. Be the source of encouragement in every situation I face. Stand up for me when I'm accused and mistreated. Fill me with grace so I can forgive with a pure heart. Your love is enough.

Amen.

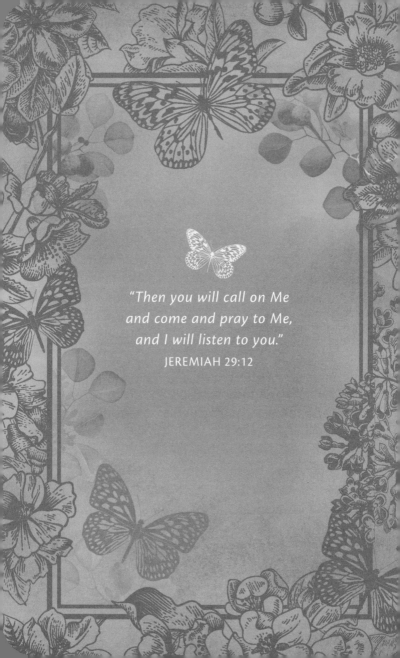

"*Then you will call on Me
and come and pray to Me,
and I will listen to you.*"

JEREMIAH 29:12

PEACE AND REST

He brought me out into a spacious place;
He rescued me because He delighted in me.

PSALM 18:19

Lord,

The demands of life are pressing so hard, I can barely breathe. It's impossible to live up to the expectations hanging over my head. The more I produce, the more is required. I wake up overwhelmed and lie down at night feeling like a failure. If I keep marching at this hard pace, I'm afraid I'll collapse.

Deliver me from this struggle, Lord. Provide strength to carry on. Protect me from those who would use my time and energy for selfish gain. Give me courage to say "no" and create margin for rest. Carry me to a spacious place where I'm safe from harm. Remind me that in Your eyes, I'm enough.

You cherish and shelter me like a little child. Wash away my fear and fill me with peace.

Amen.

MORE THAN ENOUGH

And God is able to bless you abundantly,
so that in all things at all times, having all that
you will abound in every good work.

2 CORINTHIANS 9:8

Lord,

I don't want to stand by while those around me struggle and suffer. Yet without You, I have little to give. Others' burdens are too heavy to carry. The needs are too costly to pay. Heavy emotions run too deep for my words to encourage. Hard questions are beyond my wisdom to answer. I pray You would bless me so I have an overflowing amount of goodness to share.

Please provide margin in my budget so I can give more and more. Deepen my insight to understand and share Your Word. Create empathy to comfort the hurting. Develop my spiritual gifts so I'm well-equipped to serve in Your name.

Overpower my life and use me to love.

Amen.

MAKE US NEW

*Bear with each other and forgive one another
if any of you has a grievance against someone.
Forgive as the Lord forgave you.*

COLOSSIANS 3:13

Lord,

I failed. My emotions overwhelmed my self-control and I spoke words I regret. My loved one trusted me with their heart, and I betrayed that trust. No one else is to blame – the responsibility for what I've done rests on me alone. Your Spirit convicted me of sin and I'm eager to repent.

Yet Lord, this person rejected my apology. Attempts to make amends have made no difference. The more I humble myself, the more I feel punished. I'm afraid our relationship will never be the same.

Thank You for the forgiveness I find in You. You received my confession and washed me clean. Show me how to love. Mark out a path to peace for us to follow. Restore us to one another.

Amen.

TRAINED BY LOVE

No discipline seems pleasant at the time,
but painful. Later on, however, it produces
a harvest of righteousness and peace
for those who have been trained by it.

HEBREWS 12:11

Lord,

I recognize the child inside me who wants her own way. I pout and complain, resisting the loving limits You place around me.

When life is painful or difficult, I want to run away and hide. I make foolish excuses for my sin, and I resist the hard work of growing into maturity in You.

Help me to submit to Your training. As my loving Father, You are teaching me wisdom and self-control. Your Spirit is counseling my heart and mind so I can think, speak, and live like Jesus. Even as I suffer consequences for my actions, You're using the pain to reveal Your perfect goodness. Help me to trust You and follow willingly wherever You lead.

Amen.

A BEAUTIFUL SPIRIT

*Rather, [your beauty] should be that
of your inner self, the unfading beauty
of a gentle and quiet spirit, which is
of great worth in God's sight.*

1 PETER 3:4

Lord,

Lipstick is no substitute for loving words from my mouth. A manicure adds no beauty to hands that give and serve. My posture holds the most appeal when I stand firmly in the faith. I could buy the latest fashions, but You clothe me in Christ Himself (Galatians 3:27)! I pray to reflect You, Lord, instead of just a fading image in a mirror.

Bear Your fruit of gentleness in my life. Help me to respond to antagonism with a soft answer. Soothe my temper so I give the grace I've received from You.

When I'm stressed, help me to remember Your promises. Quiet me like a little child who trusts her Father. Reveal Your beauty in me.

Amen.

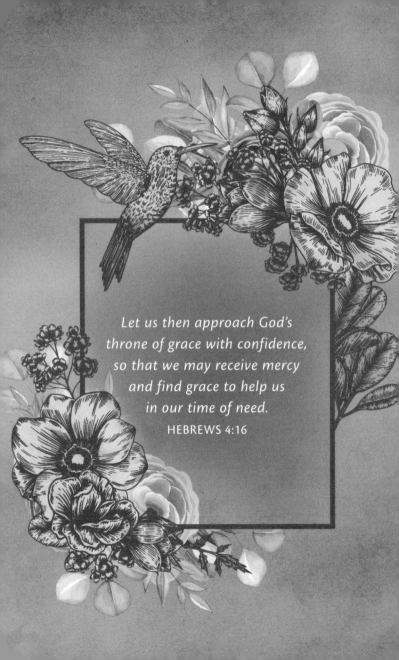

Let us then approach God's
throne of grace with confidence,
so that we may receive mercy
and find grace to help us
in our time of need.

HEBREWS 4:16

ALL EYES ON YOU

Am I now trying to win the approval of human beings, or of God? Or am I trying to please people? If I were still trying to please people, I would not be a servant of Christ.

GALATIANS 1:10

Lord,

In my insecurity, I hunger for affirmation. I'm eager to hear that I'm attractive and interesting. Useful and needed. Skilled and talented. I want to feel wanted, and I'm crushed if my hard work goes unappreciated.

Yet by striving for approval, I become a people-pleaser. I'm tempted to be fake and sacrifice my integrity. I submit to the will of others rather than You. Instead of exalting Your name, I earn praise for myself.

Be glorified in my life, Lord. "[Jesus] must become greater; I must become less" (John 3:30). Make me willing to surrender my reputation to love and serve You with all my heart. May my every thought, word, and action give You delight.

Amen.

SATISFIED BY JESUS

For the love of money is a root of all kinds of evil. Some people, eager for money, have wandered from the faith and pierced themselves with many griefs.

1 TIMOTHY 6:10

Lord,

You know the cravings of my heart. I'm tempted to find security in my income and bank account. I'm attracted to new possessions and experiences that money can buy. I compare myself to others who gain the material things of this world. My affections are torn between loving You and loving money.

Spare me the grief of a divided heart. Help me to devote myself fully to Jesus. Teach me to value my heavenly treasure above anything I could buy today. Let me keep money in its proper place as a tool to meet my needs and bless others in Your name.

Keep me full of faith and pure in heart.

Amen.

TRUSTING YOUR LOVE

*May the God of hope fill you with all joy
and peace as you trust in Him, so that
you may overflow with hope
by the power of the Holy Spirit.*

ROMANS 15:13

Lord,

From the moment You connected our lives, my loved one has held my heart. Together, we celebrate important milestones. We share tears and laughter. We built trust and hold one another's hopes and fears. Since You created our relationship, I've never been the same. My heart is breaking as I watch self-destructive choices make a wreck of my dear one's life. A stubborn attitude rejects Your wisdom and puts distance between us. The future seems dark.

Give me assurance that You hear my prayers. Refresh my hope that You're working in ways I cannot see. Give me strength to release my worries into Your hands and trust You completely.

Your goodness and love never fail.

Amen.

YOUR WONDERFUL WORK

*I praise You because I am fearfully and
wonderfully made; Your works are
wonderful, I know that full well.*

PSALM 139:14

Lord,

I confess that this body doesn't feel wonderful. I suffer
weakness and pain. My skin makes no secret of my age.
No clothing can disguise the flaws in my figure. In this
world that celebrates fitness and beauty, the mirror is
my enemy. I want to praise You as Your creation, but I
struggle to see the good in what You've made.

Help me to see myself through Your eyes. Renew my
mind so I celebrate Your works – the gift of my senses,
breath in my lungs, and strength to work and move – so
You receive the glory You deserve.

Set me free from self-hatred that diminishes my life
and denies Your love. Use every part of me to worship
You and love in Your name.

Amen.

A HUMBLE HEART

All of you, clothe yourselves with humility toward one another, because, "God opposes the proud but shows favor to the humble."

1 PETER 5:5

Lord,

In my arrogance, I secretly want to be in charge. I've mapped out an efficient path to achieve our goals. It's been proven I can solve problems and brainstorm creative ideas. I don't feel confident in the abilities of those around me. It's difficult to wait on others and put their plans and priorities ahead of my own.

Give me a humble heart like Jesus, who "did not come to be served, but to serve" (Matthew 20:28). Teach me to show respect. Open my eyes to see both the strengths in others and the weaknesses in myself.

Hold me back from forcing my ideas and opinions on everyone else. I want to listen, honor, and love with all my heart like You.

Amen.

The LORD is near
to all who call on Him,
to all who call
on Him in truth.

PSALM 145:18

JESUS UNDERSTANDS

For we do not have a high priest who is unable to empathize with our weaknesses, but we have one who has been tempted in every way, just as we are – yet He did not sin.

Lord,

You know what it's like to be a human being just like me. In my weakness I'm tempted all the time. Anger and impatience stir up words I regret.

I spend what You provide on impulsive desires. I rest too long and work too little. Love of self overrides love of others. Sin "crouches at my door" all the time (Genesis 4:7).

Thank You for grace that understands my struggle to do what's right. In Your compassion, give me strength to overcome temptation. Give power by Your Spirit to obey Your Word. Help me to follow Your perfect example of holiness and love at all times.

Amen.

YOUR PERFECT WORDS

[The serpent] said to the woman,
"Did God really say, 'You must not eat
from any tree in the garden'?"

GENESIS 3:1

Lord,

Your Word is trustworthy and true. It tells me You're always with me. It promises that nothing can separate me from Your love. Your Word gives assurance that my sins are forgiven and my future with You is secure.

Through the Scriptures You also tell me what's right. They instruct me in purity, integrity, and Your call to love others as myself. You are faithful to lead where I should go.

The enemy corrupts Your words so I believe destructive lies. He wants me to doubt Your love and mercy. Dressing up evil to look like good, he tempts me to sin. Protect me from his schemes so I remain faithful to You. Make me strong so I trust and obey You always.

Amen.

UNFAILING LOVE

Who shall separate us from the love of Christ?
Shall trouble or hardship or persecution or
famine or nakedness or danger or sword?

ROMANS 8:35

Lord,

I've been walking this hard and painful road for so long. Grief holds me on the edge of tears. When one struggle passes, another difficulty takes its place. Friends have left me alone and unseen. Hope hangs by a thread as I wait for You to provide.

Will You shine Your love in this darkness today? Help me to walk through the valley with courage since You promise to be with me through it all (Psalm 23:4).

I want to take hold of the "inexpressible and glorious joy" (1 Peter 1:8) You give to those who believe in You. I praise You that today's hurt will be tomorrow's testimony of Your love in my life. Thank You for never letting me go.

Amen.

PERFECT REST

The LORD is my shepherd, I lack nothing.
He makes me lie down in green pastures,
He leads me beside quiet waters,
He refreshes my soul.

PSALM 23:1-3

Lord,

The demands on my time, my energy, and my attention keep me rushing and working every hour of the day. Loved ones need help and care. Tasks and chores are never done. I feel if I let down my guard for a moment, everything will fall apart. The pressure to keep up is wearing me down and stealing my joy.

This frenzy of activity is not the life You designed me to live. You call me to be a woman of peace who carries Your "easy yoke" on my shoulders instead of heavy burdens of my own making (Matthew 11:30). Today, take my hand in Yours and lead me to rest. Show me what to set aside. Teach me to say "no" to commitments outside of Your perfect will.

Refresh my soul with Your tender love as I quiet myself and seek Your face.

Amen.

NOT MY OWN

*You are not your own; you were bought
at a price. Therefore honor God
with your bodies.*

1 CORINTHIANS 6:19-20

Lord,

Through Christ, You created all things (John 1:3). The life in my body is a work of Your hands. I was made with purpose and intent – You chose me before You crafted the world (Ephesians 1:4). Jesus purchased my life by giving up His own. You called me by name, I am Yours.

I want every part of me to bring glory to You. May I remain "pure and lovely" in my words, thoughts, and sexual practices (Philippians 4:8-9). Give me self-control to avoid pornographic, immoral entertainment.

Help me to cherish intimacy as a beautiful gift for marriage alone. Teach me to show sincere friendship instead of flirting to get attention. Be honored in my eating and drinking, working and resting, and loving and living each day.

Amen.

Rejoice always, pray continually,
give thanks in all circumstances;
for this is God's will for you
in Christ Jesus.

1 THESSALONIANS 5:16-18

TELLING THE TRUTH

Therefore each of you must put off falsehood
and speak truthfully to your neighbor,
for we are all members of one body.

EPHESIANS 4:25

Lord,

You know the times I fail to keep my promises. I make mistakes that cause pain and harm to those around me. Poor judgment leads to foolish choices with painful consequences. Embarrassed by my failings, I'm tempted to make up excuses or deny what I've done.

Give me the courage to take responsibility for my actions. Keep me soft and humble so I confess my sins and make amends to those I've hurt. Strengthen me to do the heart-work needed to repent and grow. Teach me to be transparent and real in my relationships.

Make me a faithful woman of my word so I'm worthy of trust. Your love and truth have never failed. May I walk in Your integrity always.

Amen.

WONDERFUL WORDS

How sweet are Your words to my taste, sweeter than honey to my mouth! Your statutes are my heritage forever; they are the joy of my heart.

PSALM 119:103, 111

Lord,

Lingering over coffee with a dear friend is a lovely way to spend an afternoon. Curling up with a book and a blanket is refreshing after a busy week. A stack of heartfelt greeting cards makes my birthday special, and a sweet compliment lifts my spirits. Words – both written and spoken – are a gift to my heart.

Yet no matter how clever or kind, no words compare to Yours. The message of Your gospel introduced me to Jesus. The truth of Your Word transforms my thoughts and guides my actions. In my pain, You speak words of healing and hope.

You lead me as a Shepherd by Your faithful, loving voice. Your words are my life and joy.

Amen.

ARMED FOR BATTLE

Put on the full armor of God, so that you can take your stand against the devil's schemes.

EPHESIANS 6:11

Lord,

Attacks from the enemy feel relentless. I want to pray and read the Bible, but distractions sabotage my time with You.

When I step up to serve, I'm overwhelmed by fear and insecurity. Little irritations somehow explode into major arguments with the ones I love. The enemy feeds my pride, steals my peace, and tempts me to sin. I need Your help to stand against his schemes.

Give me a solid footing on Your truth. Teach me how to dress in Your armor so I'm confident in who I am as Your child. Shield me from doubt as I put my trust in You. Let my righteousness shine like a star in the sky against the darkness of this world (Philippians 2:15). You are my hope and strength.

Amen.

WALKING WITH YOU

*Give careful thought to the paths for your feet
and be steadfast in all your ways.*

PROVERBS 4:26

Lord,

In this beautiful world You made, there is much to enjoy and experience. I welcome new friendships. I'm eager to take on a challenge and try new things.

My community offers countless ways to work, to volunteer, and to join in exciting activities. Yet if I say "yes" to every voice calling my name, I'll exhaust myself and lose sight of what's most important.

Help me to know Your "good, pleasing, and perfect will" for my life (Romans 12:2). Give me self-control to wait, pray, and seek advice before I step into new commitments. Keep me steady so my emotions don't rule my decisions. Provide wisdom to know when to work or rest, take a risk or move with caution.

I want to follow wherever You lead.

Amen.

THE AFTERMATH OF ANGER

An angry person stirs up conflict, and a hot-tempered person commits many sins.

PROVERBS 29:22

Lord,

Anger unleashed an attack on my heart. Harsh words accused me of bad choices and terrible motives. I felt torn apart. In the aftermath, my emotions are a tangle of fear and confusion. I wonder, *Did I deserve that treatment? Will I be rejected forever? Can I trust again? What do I do now?* The relationship is damaged and the hurt runs deep.

Meet me in this pain, Lord. If I caused offense, give me humility to make it right. Hold me back from taking revenge or retaliating with anger of my own. Draw me close for comfort. Heal the wounds I'm suffering. Give strength to forgive and wisdom to protect myself from future harm. " … You, LORD, are a shield around me, my glory, the One who lifts my head high" (Psalm 3:3).

Amen.

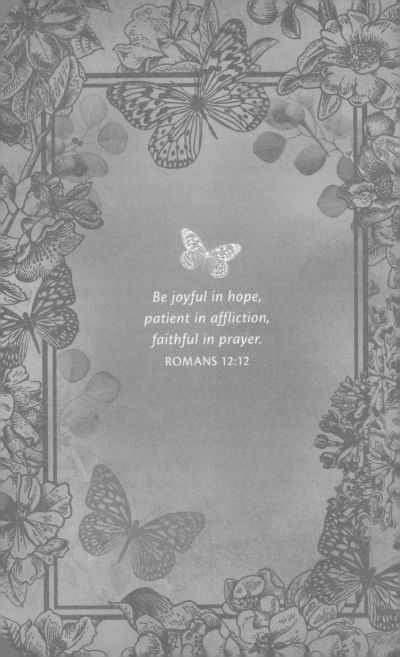

*Be joyful in hope,
patient in affliction,
faithful in prayer.*

ROMANS 12:12

FIRM IN THE FAITH

*Consider it pure joy, my brothers and sisters,
whenever you face trials of many kinds,
because you know that the testing of
your faith produces perseverance.*

JAMES 1:2-3

Lord,

I'm barely hanging on. Pain and trouble have changed my life so much, it will never look the same. I want to move forward, but impossible barriers block my path. You promise You are with me. You love me. You're my "refuge and strength, an ever-present help in trouble" (Psalm 46:1). Yet while I know You're my faithful God, I still feel alone and afraid.

I want to pass this test of my faith. Give me strength to keep believing in Your goodness. Sustain my hope that rescue is on its way. Make me so sure of Your love that I carry on with confidence and joy. Produce perseverance that overcomes doubt and despair.

Keep me close to You.

Amen.

SAVED BY GRACE

For it is by grace you have been saved,
through faith – and this is not from yourselves,
it is the gift of God – not by works, so that
no one can boast.

EPHESIANS 2:8-9

Lord,

I know how to play the part of a religious person. I can recite a script of spiritual words and platitudes. Hiding my true thoughts and feelings, I can put on a smile and keep the peace. When help is needed, I do my part. Others say my life looks pure and clean. Yet if I depend on my image and behavior to save my soul, all is lost.

Once more, write Your gospel on my heart. Establish true faith and sincere love for You in my life. Forgive me for diminishing the work of Jesus by trying to earn Your great salvation.

Overwhelm me with the beauty of Your goodness and grace.

Amen.

LOVING COMFORT

*[The Father of compassion] comforts us
in all our troubles, so that we can comfort
those in any trouble with the comfort
we ourselves receive from God.*

2 CORINTHIANS 1:3-4

Lord,

You brought me from darkness into light. The medicine of Your love healed the wounds in my heart. Your wisdom cleared up my confusion. When I was rejected, You stood by my side. You saved me from harm, provided for my needs, and set me free from sin. You fill me with joy and peace too wonderful to understand.

I want my friends and family to know Your comfort, too. Give me words to tell the story of Your love. Show me how to give and serve just like Jesus cares for me. Fill me with compassion for suffering so I can pray, encourage, and carry others' burdens in Your name.

Use me to reveal Your goodness to everyone.

Amen.

COUNTING MY BLESSINGS

Let them give thanks to the LORD for His unfailing love ... Let them sacrifice thank offerings and tell of His works with songs of joy.

PSALM 107:21-22

Lord,

Apart from You I'm never satisfied. I dream of a spacious home with beautiful curb appeal. Other women's clothes outshine what hangs in my closet. My income struggles to keep pace with life's expenses. Other families seem happy and carefree compared to my own. As I sink into discontent, I find myself counting my losses instead of the blessings You've given.

Shift my perspective so I can see Your goodness in my life. You delivered me from trouble, provided for my needs, and healed my wounds. You listen to my prayers and never leave my side. Set free from guilt and fear, I face the future with hope. You are worthy of all my praise forever!

Thank You for Your love.

Amen.

SHINING YOUR LIGHT

"In the same way, let Your light shine before others, that they may see Your good deeds and glorify Your Father in heaven."

MATTHEW 5:16

Lord,

You reveal Your love through the goodness of people in my life. A little child's hug around my neck is a taste of Your tenderness. When I'm thoughtless, a friend's patience and forgiveness lets me know Your grace.

Artists, builders, and musicians display Your beautiful creativity. Writers and teachers – empowered by Your Spirt – untangle the "deep things of God" hidden in Your Word (1 Corinthians 2:10). You reveal Your wisdom, truth, and love through others so I can walk in Your light.

Teach me to do what's good and right. Show me how to use Your spiritual gifts so I can give, help, and serve beyond my own ability. Weave Your love through my life so Jesus is seen in me.

Amen.

May my prayer be set before You
like incense; may the lifting
up of my hands be like
the evening sacrifice.

PSALM 141:2

NEVER THE SAME

Therefore, if anyone is in Christ, the new creation has come: The old has gone, the new is here!

2 CORINTHIANS 5:17

Lord,

I can't imagine who I would be without You. Would I carry bitterness for failed dreams and plans? Would my old, selfish habits damage relationships beyond repair? In the face of trouble, would I run in fear or sink into depression? I'm grateful for the freedom I know today – You loved me and called me from darkness into Your wonderful light (1 Peter 2:9).

May I never forget who I am in You. Keep me from slipping into shame by doubting Your forgiveness. Empower me to resist the enemy and overcome temptation. Continue to transform my heart so I'm motivated by love in all I do and say.

Be my source of joy that completely satisfies. Thank You for making me new in Your love.

Amen.

THE "SCHOOL" OF SCRIPTURE

*All Scripture is God-breathed and is useful
for teaching, rebuking, correcting and training
in righteousness, so that the servant of God may
be thoroughly equipped for every good work.*

2 TIMOTHY 3:16-17

Lord,

You call me Your daughter, friend, and servant. I'm here, ready to serve however You ask. Equip me by Your Word to answer Your call and love others in Your name.

Teach me what's true so I can discern what's real around me. Challenge my thinking and correct the errors in my understanding and attitude. Convict me of selfishness and pride so I'm pure in heart. Equip me with knowledge so I can handle Your Word with wisdom and care. Use Scripture to teach obedience in every aspect of my life.

Thank You for preparing good works in advance for me to do (Ephesians 2:10). May I be a worthy servant who gives You joy.

Amen.

LOVING AND BELIEVING

And this is His command: to believe in the name of His Son, Jesus Christ, and to love one another as He commanded us. The one who keeps God's commands lives in Him, and He in them.

1 John 3:23-24

Lord,

Life is found in faith and love. I believe in Jesus as my Savior, Friend, and King. Today, deepen my confidence in His work on the cross that covers my sin.

Renew my hope, knowing He will overcome evil in the world. Help me to live abundantly by trusting in Jesus for everything.

As I grow in faith, let Your love live in me. May the compassion I receive from You flow out in mercy to others. May I share Your gifts to me with those in need. Give me a gracious heart that forgives as I've been forgiven. Fill my life with Your power and presence.

Amen.

A FORGIVING HEART

"But to you who are listening I say: Love your enemies, do good to those who hate you, bless those who curse you, pray for those who mistreat you."

LUKE 6:27

Lord,

As gossip reaches my ears, the insults pierce like a knife. The accusations are unfair. The rumors are based on lies. No matter what I say or do, I can't restore what's been taken from me. I'm under attack with no defense. I wish I could cut my enemies down to size and get the payback I deserve.

Yet I do not want anger to consume my heart. Help me to quiet my thoughts and trust in Your care. Give me deep compassion so I can forgive as You've forgiven me. Show me how to respond to hatred with love, curses with blessings, and evil with goodness. Draw my enemies to Yourself by Your mercy and kindness.

Amen.

ALL IS WELL

I have learned the secret of being content in any and every situation, whether well fed or hungry, whether living in plenty or in want.

PHILIPPIANS 4:12

Lord,

By this age and stage of my life, I expected more. I assumed my relationships would be happy and fulfilling. My career would use my talents and provide generously for my needs. Confident and well-traveled, I'd be a woman of the world. Yet I find myself living a simple, ordinary existence.

I'm stressed by difficult people and my own limitations. Dreams have taken a back seat to the daily grind. Will I count my blessings or resent what's missing in my life?

I pray for the sweet gift of contentment. Fill me with unconditional joy. Grow my faith that You use every trial for good in the end. Keep me from selfishness that is never satisfied. Your love and grace are enough.

Amen.

If we confess our sins,
He is faithful and just
and will forgive us our
sins and purify us from
all unrighteousness.

1 JOHN 1:9

THE PRECIOUS PRODIGAL

Let's have a feast and celebrate.
For this son of mine was dead and is
alive again; he was lost and is found.

LUKE 15:23-24

Lord,

My loved one is far from You. Deceived and confused, they ignore Your Word and Your ways. They have separated themselves from believers, taking up with those "who call evil good and good evil" (Isaiah 5:20). Fear, frustration, and sadness are taking hold in their life. They need You to bring them back into Your light.

Jesus came to seek and to save the lost (Luke 19:10). Pursue the heart of the one I love. Open their eyes to see You. Humble their heart to admit their need and ask for Your kindness and mercy.

Move them to pray, turn from sin, and surrender their life to Your control. Restore what is broken, heal every wound, and give them eternal life through Jesus.

Amen.

READY TO RESIST

Be alert and of sober mind. Your enemy the devil
prowls around like a roaring lion looking
for someone to devour. Resist him,
standing firm in the faith, because you know
that the family of believers throughout the world
is undergoing the same kind of sufferings.

1 PETER 5:8-9

Lord,

The enemy is determined to bring me down. He stirs up fear to steal my sleep and paralyze me with anxiety. He whispers flattery to puff me up with pride and arrogance. He twists the truth so I doubt Your Word.

He confuses my thinking, blinding me to Your love and goodness. He brings trouble and distraction wherever I go.

Give me strength to resist the enemy today. Fill me with courageous faith that won't be shaken. Make me sure of Your constant love. Help me to endure without giving in or giving up. May I be faithful always.

Amen.

FAITH LIKE A CHILD

*"Look at the birds of the air; they do not sow
or reap or store away in barns, and yet
your heavenly Father feeds them.
Are you not much more valuable than they?"*

MATTHEW 6:26

Lord,

Strong. Decisive. Independent. Capable. Prepared. I'm expected to be these and more as so much responsibility rests on my shoulders.

Others count on me for help and answers every day. I'm afraid I'll lose my nerve. What if I fail? What will happen when my strength or resources are simply not enough? I care for others, but who will care for me?

Forgive this proud self-sufficiency that denies my need for You. Teach me to be like a little child who trusts You, follows You, and rests in Your love. Renew my mind so I better understand how You provide for Your own.

Please quiet my fears, grow my faith, and fill me with Your peace.

Amen.

BUSY OR BLESSED

[Martha] had a sister called Mary, who sat at the Lord's feet listening to what He said. But Martha was distracted by all the preparations that had to be made.

LUKE 10:39-40

Lord,

It is a joy to serve the people in my life. Helping, showing hospitality, and carrying others' burdens lets me put Your love in action. My days are full as the list of needs is never fully met. Yet I can let the demands on my time and attention take my eyes off You.

I hear You calling me to sit at Your feet and listen to Your voice. Open my hands to receive Your gift of rest. Give me self-control to quiet myself and study Your Word. Teach me humility so I cancel my attempts to be all things to all people.

My heart wants to abide in You, pray without ceasing, and seek Your loving face.

Amen.

PUTTING YOU FIRST

"Anyone who loves their father or mother more than Me is not worthy of Me; anyone who loves their son or daughter more than Me is not worthy of Me."

MATTHEW 10:37

Lord,

My family needs me. Our lives are woven so tightly together, they feel like a part of me. When they hurt, I feel wounded. Each time they are blessed, I'm filled with joy. My focus is consumed with helping and caring for them every day.

Yet I want to love You with all my heart and soul and strength (Deuteronomy 6:5). I need Your Spirit to guard my heart from putting anyone – even my precious family – in Your place. Help me to do Your will instead of striving for their approval. Let me trust You to meet their needs instead of placing that entire load on my own shoulders.

Take first place in my heart.

Amen.

Search for the LORD and
for His strength;
continually seek Him.

1 CHRONICLES 16:11

AN OPEN TABLE

Keep on loving one another as brothers and sisters. Do not forget to show hospitality to strangers, for by so doing some people have shown hospitality to angels without knowing it.

HEBREWS 13:1-2

Lord,

By the work of Your Spirit, a warm welcome and a meal can change a life. Teach me how to use my home to express Your love and care. Keep my door open to those who need a friend.

Fill each room with peace and joy to create a place of refuge. Open my heart so I gladly share my space with those who need Your kindness.

Show me the true meaning of hospitality. Keep me flexible so I can respond quickly to the needs around me. Make me humble so I design my home to serve and not to impress. As You open my doors, open hearts to Your love.

Amen.

TRUE BEAUTY

Charm is deceptive, and beauty is fleeting;
but a woman who fears the Lord is to be praised.

PROVERBS 31:30

Lord,

In my heart, I'm eager to earn the praise of family and friends. I crave a reward and a "well done" after a hard day's work. I've grown skilled in hiding my true self under a pleasing smile. In my efforts to keep people happy, I focus on my appearance. I compromise to keep the peace. I live up to their expectations instead of Yours.

Instead, set the standard for all I do and say. Help me to obey Your Word, even if I must stand alone. Make me an authentic woman who worships with abandon, celebrates the good news of the gospel, and loves "the least of these" (Matthew 25:40) without apology.

Fill me with the true beauty of a quiet and gentle spirit (1 Peter 3:4).

Amen.

WILLING TO WORK

Whatever you do, work at it with all your heart,
as working for the Lord, not for human masters,
since you know that you will receive
an inheritance from the Lord as a reward.

COLOSSIANS 3:23-24

Lord,

My hard work is taken for granted. I show integrity while others cheat and get ahead. After taking initiative to learn and grow, my abilities remain overlooked. Instead of a reward, I have little to show for my effort. I'm losing motivation and I'm tempted to quit.

Lift my eyes higher so I see You as the ultimate authority over my life. Give me joy in working and serving by knowing You're pleased. Energize me with confidence that You hold priceless, eternal rewards in Your hands.

Forgive me for pride that craves human praise. Make me selfless and humble like Jesus. May I work for You with a pure and willing heart.

Amen.

STRENGTH TO SERVE

Let us not become weary in doing good,
for at the proper time we will reap
a harvest if we do not give up.

GALATIANS 6:9

Lord,

As Your daughter I'm called to love. My help is needed each day. Others depend on my hard work. If I choose to please myself, my friends, peers, and family pay the price. My "good deeds" are meant to fulfill my purpose, shine Your light, and bring You glory (Matthew 5:16).

While Your calling on my life is an honor, I become weary. It hurts to be unappreciated. The day's list of tasks feels long while the hours seem far too short to accomplish them. When my efforts bear little fruit, I lose motivation to carry on.

Refresh my energy and rekindle my passion to serve, Lord. Give me hope in the harvest that's to come. Keep me faithful to the end.

Amen.

FORGIVEN AND LOVED

*"I, even I, am He who blots out your
transgressions, for My own sake,
and remembers your sins no more."*

ISAIAH 43:25

Lord,

Your love is overwhelming. My stubborn, rebellious heart was met with mercy and love. While I was still deep in my sin, You gave Your own Son to save my soul. The memories of my wrongdoing are fresh in my mind, yet You call me clean and whole, new and redeemed. You are worthy of my praise forever!

Yet even as I receive this beautiful grace, I can struggle to offer it myself. Others' actions and attitudes stir up my anger. I dwell on the offense and hold a grudge. Fill me with compassion that forgives as I've been forgiven.

Let me view others through Your eyes of perfect love. Keep me humble and merciful in spirit for the sake of Jesus' name.

Amen.

Is anyone among you in trouble?
Let them pray. Is anyone happy?
Let them sing songs of praise.

JAMES 5:13

JOYFUL OR JEALOUS

A heart at peace gives life to the body,
but envy rots the bones.

PROVERBS 14:30

Lord,

Life hasn't turned out as I expected. Others shine in the spotlight while I feel invisible to everyone. Doors of opportunity have closed in my face. Finances keep me from experiencing what the world has to offer, while friends move from one adventure to another.

Others seem cherished while I feel unwanted and alone. Jealousy is putting down bitter roots in my spirit. I'm losing hope for tomorrow.

I need a new heart, Lord. "Restore to me the joy of my salvation" (Psalm 51:12). Refresh my gratitude for Your lavish gifts of mercy, help, and love. Let me celebrate Your unique plan and will for my life.

Keep me from comparing myself to others so I view myself through Your eyes alone. Fill me with peace as I believe and trust in You.

Amen.

A CRY FOR HELP

You, LORD, hear the desire of the afflicted;
You encourage them, and You listen to their cry.

PSALM 10:17

Lord,

My loved one is suffering. Pain and fear have taken hold, stealing hope for tomorrow. Faith is wearing away as they wait for relief.

They wonder, *Does God hear my prayers? Why is He leading me through this dark valley? Will I ever feel well and whole again?* No longer confident in Your goodness, they are losing their way in the darkness.

Use me to comfort and encourage. Show me when to speak or simply listen. Let my help ease the burden they carry. Protect my own heart from worry and doubt as I walk by their side. I want to shine Your light and show the love of Jesus in all I do and say.

Reveal Yourself as the mighty Deliverer who makes all things new.

Amen.

A LOVE LIKE YOURS

*Accept one another, then, just as
Christ accepted you, in order
to bring praise to God.*

ROMANS 15:7

Lord,

As a daughter in Your church family, You call me to love like Jesus. He is full of patience and grace. He looks past a person's outer appearance to cherish their heart (1 Samuel 16:7).

Jesus offers continual prayer, encouragement, and help to keep us close to You. His great desire is for His children to love and live as one.

Give me a tender heart toward those around me. Keep me from pointing fingers and judging others' mistakes. Set me free from a proud and critical spirit that wounds and pushes others away. Help me to be sensitive so I can "rejoice with those who rejoice" and "mourn with those who mourn" (Romans 12:15).

Make me a woman who shows honor, kindness, and sincere love to everyone.

Amen.

AN EXAMPLE TO FOLLOW

Follow God's example, therefore, as dearly loved children and walk in the way of love.

EPHESIANS 5:1-2

Lord,

Relationships are complicated. Feelings are hurt by a careless word. It's difficult to know who to trust. Helpful acts can be manipulation in disguise. Selfishness and pride tear loved ones apart. As human beings, we're slow to listen and quick to become angry. We need You to teach us to love.

Thank You for the example of Jesus. He opened His arms to children. He honored those who the culture despised. When His friends were stubborn or slow to understand, He showed patience and grace. Betrayal was met with mercy. Hunger was satisfied and wounds were healed. All He did, He did for love.

Help me to follow Your beautiful example for my life. Pattern my heart and mind after Jesus'. May I walk in the way of love.

Amen.

BUILDING MY HOUSE

The wise woman builds her house, but with her own hands the foolish one tears hers down.

PROVERBS 14:1

Lord,

A home is more than a house with walls and windows and doors. Home is meant to be a refuge. A place of rest and comfort. A safe space to express feelings and experience unconditional love. Home is where I can draw close to dear friends and family, and it's my personal place to abide with You.

Yet in my foolishness and sin, I can tear down the beautiful gift of home that You've given. Anger and harsh words can send my loved ones running for cover. Selfishness shuts the door to sharing and hospitality.

A hard, unforgiving heart allows bitterness to divide my family. Today I pray for help to love well, speak wisely, and build my home on the foundation of Your Word. Dwell with us, Lord.

Amen.

Give all your worries and cares to God, for He cares about you.

1 PETER 5:7

YOUR PERFECT PLANS

In their hearts humans plan their course,
but the LORD establishes their steps.

PROVERBS 16:9

Lord,

My plans have crumbled to dust at my feet. Those hopes and dreams were dear to my heart. I've been waiting and working to gain blessing, joy, and good fruit for my effort. But now the future seems blank. I'm discouraged and don't know which way to go.

Yet Your Spirit reminds me that You are God and I am not. I can work and strive, but You have the last word over every detail of my life. No matter how much I want my own way, it's Your will that is truly good, pleasing, and perfect (Romans 12:2).

Help me to trust You. Your love is constant. Your ways and thoughts are higher than my own. And Your plans for me hold glorious hope and a future with You.

Amen.

LISTENING FOR YOU

*The Lord came and stood there, calling as
at the other times, "Samuel! Samuel!"
Then Samuel said, "Speak,
for Your servant is listening."*

1 Samuel 3:10

Lord,

How many times have You called my name, but I was too worried or distracted to notice? You wanted to offer direction, but I was busy making my own plans. You spoke words of comfort, but I numbed my sorrows with entertainment, food, or sleep. I closed my ears to Your Spirit's correction. As Your dearly loved sheep, I should know my Shepherd's voice (John 10:27).

Help me to quiet my thoughts and focus on Your words. "My God, whom I praise, do not remain silent" (Psalm 109:1). Instead, teach me Your ways. Expose my attitudes and sin so I can repent. Declare Your calling on my life so I can serve and love in Your name. I'm listening.

Amen.

TRUE OR FALSE

*"Watch out for false prophets. They come
to you in sheep's clothing, but inwardly they
are ferocious wolves. By their fruit
you will recognize them."*

MATTHEW 7:15-16

Lord,

Your church is beautiful. In Your family, I belong. It offers a place to learn Your ways and live out Your purpose for my life. Your church is a taste of the worship and eternal community I'll know in heaven.

Yet destructive liars work their way in among Your people. They burden me with legalistic rules that deny Your grace. They twist the Scriptures to confuse my thinking. These "wolves" exploit Your children for their own gain. They stir up division and doubt.

Protect me, Lord, from their schemes. Give me discernment to separate the false from the true. Put trustworthy, loving leaders over my life. Make me mature in my understanding of You. Keep me always close and faithful.

Amen.

SEARCHING FOR GOD

"You will seek Me and find Me when you seek Me with all your heart."

JEREMIAH 29:13

Lord,

I need You desperately. Without You, I have no wisdom or understanding. Hope is crippled by despair. Sin takes hold so I turn from Your ways and hurt the ones I'm called to love. When I drift away from You, I become lost, broken, and afraid.

I want to find You, Father. Reveal Yourself through Your magnificent creation. Speak through Your Word and Your people. Keep me persistent in prayer until I hear Your voice.

Help me to let go of my own desires so I am satisfied by You alone. Day and night, teach me to abide in You so I can bear fruit (John 15:4) and love You with an undivided heart. Draw near to me as I draw near to You (James 4:8).

Amen.

FAITH TO WAIT

*Wait for the LORD; be strong and
take heart and wait for the LORD.*

PSALM 27:14

Lord,

I've lifted up the same request to You more times than I can count. I feel exhausted from carrying this heavy burden for so long. Hard work, creativity, and others' advice have failed to move me even one step forward. I feel trapped in this difficulty with no hope of change.

I want to believe You, Lord, when You say You're here. Help me to trust You're working in ways You'll reveal at the perfect time. Fill me with courage to stand firm in the face of the enemy's lies and temptation to give up and quit. Bring Your comfort and encouragement so I "rejoice always, pray without ceasing," and give thanks in everything (1 Thessalonians 5:16-18).

I know You are good. Give me strength in the waiting today.

Amen.

"*I tell you, you can pray for anything, and if you believe that you've received it, it will be yours.*"

MARK 11:24

WALKING IN THE TRUTH

*It gave me great joy when some believers came
and testified about your faithfulness to
the truth, telling how you continue to walk
in it. I have no greater joy than to hear
that my children are walking in the truth.*

3 JOHN 3:3-4

Lord,

My heart's desire is to live by Your truth. Shape my views by the Bible, rather than public opinion. Shield me from those who would persuade me to deny what's right. Give strength so I can stand firm when I'm tempted to go my own way. Let me be known for unshakeable confidence in the Word.

Deepen my knowledge of Your truth each day. Teach me to be still and hear Your voice as my Shepherd. Give me diligence to meditate and study Your words.

Provide godly preachers and counselors to instruct my heart. Enable me to walk in obedience until I see Your face.

Amen.

SEEK AND BELIEVE

*And without faith it is impossible to please God,
because anyone who comes to Him must believe
that He exists and that He rewards those
who earnestly seek Him.*

HEBREWS 11:6

Lord,

My heart's desire is to please You. Yet my faith is small. I struggle with doubt, and I falter in my determination to seek You.

Temporary struggles make me forget Your eternal promises. Renew my confidence in Your love by Your Spirit. Rekindle my passion to know You more and more.

Open my eyes to recognize Your beauty and power displayed in the created world. Give me unshakeable trust in Your perfect Word. Teach me to pray – earnestly, constantly, honestly – believing You hear and answer.

Reward me with strong faith that hopes in You and obeys without giving up. Fill me with love for You, my Savior, King, and Friend.

Amen.

GIFTED TO SERVE

There are different kinds of gifts, but the same Spirit distributes them. There are different kinds of service, but the same Lord.

1 CORINTHIANS 12:4-5

Lord,

I see women serving as confident, articulate teachers who make Your Word come alive. Some have the sweet ability to feed the soul around their beautiful, nourishing tables.

The artistic and musical talents of Your servants take my breath away. Bold evangelists and tender helpers display Jesus right before my eyes. As I admire those who step into their spiritually-gifted callings, I secretly wonder if there's a place for me too.

Help me to trust Your promise to place Your gift inside of me. Reveal how I'm to serve and give with the Spirit's help. You created me for good works that You prepared long ago (Ephesians 2:10). Help me to discover my purpose as Your daughter. Use my life for Your glory.

Amen.

LOVING GOD, LOVING OTHERS

*And this is love: that we walk in obedience
to His commands. As you have heard from the
beginning, His command is that you walk in love.*

2 JOHN 6

Lord,

To love You means loving others. I cannot harden my heart toward people and keep a soft heart toward You.

I can't hoard Your gifts for myself while praising Your generosity. I will not find rest in Your mercy if I refuse to forgive those who hurt me. My love for You is proved by the compassion, kindness, and integrity I show to everyone.

Give me a devoted heart that loves in Your name. Reveal any hypocrisy in my life that says one thing and does another. Fill me with joy in giving, serving, and encouraging those around me. May I speak and live faithfully in Your love at all times.

Amen.

BLESSED ASSURANCE

*Whoever has the Son has life; whoever does not
have the Son of God does not have life.
I write these things to you who believe
in the name of the Son of God so that you
may know that you have eternal life.*

1 JOHN 5:12-13

Lord,

My failure seems bigger than Your grace today. Insecurity builds as I battle with sin. I secretly wonder, *Would I fight temptation if I was truly saved? Will God give up on me? Do I have the right to ask for forgiveness?*

I feel unworthy – it makes me want to hide from Your face. Thank You for telling me I'm Yours when I'm afraid and insecure. I received Your Son when I believed in His name. You forgive and forget my sins for all time (Hebrews 8:12). In You, I have eternal life that nothing can take away.

Amen.

"If you remain in Me and My words remain in you, ask whatever you wish, and it will be done for you."

JOHN 15:7

WISDOM ON THE WAY

*If any of you lacks wisdom, you should ask God,
who gives generously to all without finding fault,
and it will be given to you.*

JAMES 1:5

Lord,

I stand at a crossroads – which way should I go? Each path may hold risks or rewards, burdens or benefits. My choice will affect my future and the ones I love. In this confusion, I'm stuck and unable to move forward without Your help. I can't depend on my own wisdom since fearful thoughts and selfish desires tempt me all the time.

Give me insight to know what to do. Have compassion for my lack of knowledge and understanding. Reveal Your perfect, pleasing will so I can obey. I want to go where You take me, give what You ask of me, and learn all You want to teach me each day. Thank You for leading my life.

Amen.

THE GIFT OF FRIENDS

The righteous choose their friends carefully,
but the way of the wicked leads them astray.

PROVERBS 12:26

Lord,

It's not just the young who fall victim to peer pressure. Friends' cravings for material things stir up greed and jealousy in my heart. Consumed with success, others can tempt me to sacrifice relationships at the altar of my goals.

My social circle can lure me into gossip, complaining, and insulting the ones I love most. I need godly friends who bring out my best and set an example to follow.

Keep me from settling for destructive relationships when I'm lonely. Give me courage to speak the truth and do what's right, even if I stand alone. Show Your kindness and mercy by giving me friends with deep faith and authentic love. Use my sisters in Christ to mark out a path of obedience and devotion to You.

Amen.

HELP HER UP, LORD

*Two are better than one, because they have
a good return for their labor: If either of
them falls down, one can help the other up.*

ECCLESIASTES 4:9-10

Lord,

You gave me a partner to run the race of faith by my
side. She prayed for my needs and carried my burdens.
Her wise insight made Your Word come alive. Her
victories over sin and Satan built my trust in Your
power. Together, we had strength.

Yet today, deep pain is shaking her confidence in
Your love. She wonders if You hear her prayers. She
finds no comfort in the Bible or the church. As she
turns to the world for help and answers, I see her wan-
dering far from You.

Instruct me in what to say and do. Use me to bring
hope as I care for her like Jesus. Enable me to help her
up by Your Spirit.

Amen.

ALL FOR JESUS

*So whether you eat or drink or whatever you do,
do it all for the glory of God.*

1 CORINTHIANS 10:31

Lord,

You offer Yourself as my Source. In You, I find strength to resist the enemy and do hard things. You provide peace in my worries and quiet rest when life is overwhelming. If I have a need, You faithfully provide. Your compassion and presence are with me every moment.

Even so, I foolishly rely on Your gifts instead of You as their giver. I use food and drink to boost my mood and energy. I escape the day's anxieties with devices and entertainment to soothe my spirit. Human voices speak as a substitute for Your perfect wisdom and affection.

Teach me to glorify You by putting my faith in You alone. Be my true comfort. Empower me with Your Spirit. Satisfy me completely with Your love.

Amen.

MY GREATEST LOVE

You make known to me the path of life;
You will fill me with joy in Your presence,
with eternal pleasures at Your right hand.

PSALM 16:11

Lord,

As a woman I long to be loved. I want to feel desired, cherished, and romanced. In my loneliness, I dream of sweet companionship that never leaves my side. It's tempting to believe that a human relationship could satisfy all the desires of my heart.

Draw me close, Lord. Remind me that no one will ever love me like You. Who else has "loved [me] with an everlasting love" and "drawn [me] with unfailing kindness" like my God? (Jeremiah 31:3). Give me such joy in Your presence that I am fully content and satisfied.

Help me to find my life in You and You alone. You are my identity and worth, my happiness and peace. Be my first love, always.

Amen.

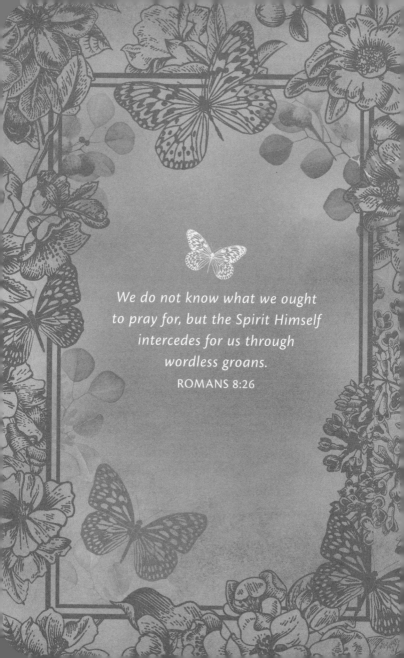

We do not know what we ought to pray for, but the Spirit Himself intercedes for us through wordless groans.

ROMANS 8:26

CHOSEN AND LOVED

You are the children of the LORD your God.
Out of all the peoples on the face of the earth,
the LORD has chosen you to be
His treasured possession.

DEUTERONOMY 14:1-2

Lord,

My life is small and ordinary. I don't attract much praise or attention. While I care for my loved ones, I often feel unappreciated and unseen. In my heart of hearts, I wonder if I make a difference. Am I unique or special? What is my true worth?

Yet when I feel insecure, You tell me I'm chosen. Treasured. Beloved. You "keep me as the apple of Your eye" (Psalm 17:8). In Your limitless love, You gave Your own Son to purchase my life forever. You listen to every prayer, You anticipate my needs, and You never leave my side. Because of You, I belong.

Thank You for giving me dignity and a life that matters.

Amen.

MY SOURCE OF STRENGTH

Some trust in chariots and some in horses,
but we trust in the name of the LORD our God.

PSALM 20:7

Lord,

I'm a strong and independent woman. My education, experience, and hard work earn respect. Friends and loved ones have my back.

My possessions and money in the bank give assurance that today's needs will be met. While these assets are a blessing, they can tempt me to forget how much I need You. Instead of trusting You, my heart grows proud. Self-sufficiency keeps me from seeking Your face.

Move in my heart to make me humble. Train my eyes to see You as the source of everything wonderful in my life. Keep me faithful in prayer for all my needs. Instead of trusting in relationships, money, or success, let me depend on Your love. "Apart from You I have no good thing" (Psalm 16:2).

Amen.

A LOVE LIKE YOURS

A father to the fatherless, a defender of widows,
is God in His holy dwelling.

PSALM 68:5

Lord,

This world values money and power, beauty and fame. We measure success by popularity and how far we can separate ourselves from poverty and suffering.

The most vulnerable among us – the orphans, disabled, displaced, and elderly – are ignored at best and exploited at worst. Yet You, Lord, hold the "least of these" (Matthew 25:40) close to Your heart.

Thank You for Your love that embraces the most lonely, helpless, and unseen among us. Instead of caring for outer appearance, You look at the heart (1 Samuel 16:7). Teach me, Father, to show compassion like You.

Use me to feed the hungry, heal the wounded, and stand for justice. Give me Christlike humility to honor all people. I want to be Your hands and feet of love in this world.

Amen.

MY CHAMPION

The LORD will fight for you;
you need only to be still.

Lord,

The battle is raging around me today. I've picked up my weapons of hard work and determination, but I can't get the upper hand no matter how hard I try. My relentless research has failed to find solutions to my problem. Despite my cries for help, no one comes to my rescue. I feel exhausted, helpless, and desperate. Without You, I have no hope.

Quiet my spirit in this fight. Move me from panic to peace as I trust in You. Be my champion against the enemies I face. Shield me from danger and give me justice that restores what's been taken from me.

Please fill me with confidence in Your power and love so that my faith is never shaken. "You are my hiding place" who will "surround me with songs of deliverance" (Psalm 32:7).

Amen.

BRINGING YOUR PEACE

If it is possible, as far as it depends on you,
live at peace with everyone.

ROMANS 12:18

Lord,

My thoughtless words leave a trail of hurt feelings behind them. I fail to listen or give my loved ones the consideration they deserve. In my forgetfulness, I break promises and let others down. I know my sin can damage the most important relationships You've built into my life.

Teach me to be a woman of peace. Use my mouth to speak words that encourage and build others up. Keep me humble so I'm quick to apologize and take responsibility for my mistakes.

Train me to listen and pray before reacting to my friends and family in anger. Silence my selfish, critical thoughts.

Help me to be kind as I work for unity with everyone around me. I want to be a peacemaker like Jesus.

Amen.

"Ask and it will be given to you;
seek and you will find;
knock and the door will
be opened to you."

LUKE 11:9

GROWING AND CHANGING

As iron sharpens iron, so one person sharpens another.

PROVERBS 27:17

Lord,

I've fallen into a rut. My habits are predictable. It's been a long time since I wrestled with deep truths or questions. My relationships are comfortable and familiar – we no longer excavate one another's emotions, ideas, or heart-needs. Instead of stretching myself and welcoming change, I've grown passive. I need a fresh challenge to pursue You with all my heart.

Sharpen me, Lord, through the example and words of other believers. Use them to point out my sin so I can repent and do what's right. Through their insight, reveal my spiritual gifts and motivate me to serve You with passion. If I'm wrong in my understanding of Your Word, provide teaching to renew my mind.

Use godly brothers and sisters to build my faith. Thank You for Your faithful work to make me like Jesus.

Amen.

A PATIENT HEART

A person's wisdom yields patience;
it is to one's glory to overlook an offense.

PROVERBS 19:11

Lord,

My loved one knows exactly which words and habits will push my buttons. I've made my needs and requests as clear as they can be, but they go ignored and disregarded. Over and over, I suffer disrespect. Interruptions. Unreasonable expectations. Broken promises and careless actions. Each offense is a brick in a wall around my heart.

Yet You've never grown weary in forgiving my sins. Each and every time I confess, You wash me clean and offer another chance to get it right. No mistakes or faults can drive You away – nothing separates me from Your love at any time (Romans 8:39). Your mercy never fails.

Fill me with Your love so I can forgive like You. Teach me patience that bears with others and refuses to hold a grudge.

Amen.

ONLY JESUS

*But when the kindness and love of God
our Savior appeared, He saved us, not
because of righteous things we had done,
but because of His mercy.*

TITUS 3:4-5

Lord,

I'm saved because of Your love and compassion. None of my good works or religious actions could pay for my salvation – life is found in Christ alone.

Yet over time I can grow passive and forget You're my source. Pride creeps in, saying I'm better than others. I can give and serve in my own strength. I can depend on my own wisdom. I can clean up my own sinful mess. I trust in my own goodness instead of all Jesus has done for me.

Give me a humble heart to depend on You. Restore my awe and gratitude for Your mercy. Teach my heart to trust in You – and only You – for righteousness, wisdom, and eternal life.

Amen.

WE'RE IN THIS TOGETHER

And let us consider how we may spur one another on toward love and good deeds.

HEBREWS 10:24

Lord,

Thank You for adopting me into Your family of believers. In Your mercy, You give us one another to help us follow You. Surround me with examples of love – men and women who put others first, serve sacrificially, and rescue those in trouble.

Provide encouragement when I'm afraid or tempted to doubt Your truth. Use mature and godly people to give accountability when I'm tempted. May Your church be a source of hope, healing, and help in my life.

Show me how to bless my brothers and sisters in Jesus. Let my words and my obedience motivate others to serve in Your name. Fill me with contagious joy and faith that shows Your love to everyone. Make us one by Your Spirit.

Amen.

FAITHFUL AND TRUE

*Then they returned ... strengthening
the disciples and encouraging them to
remain true to the faith. "We must go
through many hardships to enter
the kingdom of God," they said.*

ACTS 14:21-22

Lord,

You are faithful to tell the truth that "in this world [we] will have trouble" (John 16:33). In Your kindness, You warned me of false teachers who would try to turn me away from You.

You explained that by uniting myself to Christ, I would experience the same hatred He suffered. Your Word describes evil persecution against Your people that continues to this day. But in these difficult realities, You give me all I need.

Thank You for comfort when I'm wounded. You protect me, encourage me, and hold heavenly rewards in the end. You created the church so we could link arms and stand strong together. Hope, peace, and Your lavish love are mine every moment.

Amen.

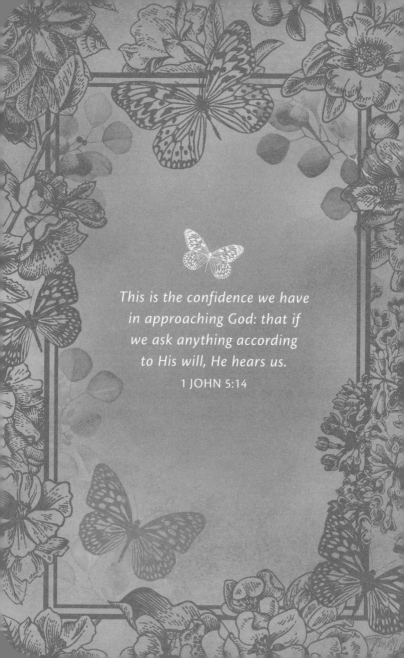

*This is the confidence we have
in approaching God: that if
we ask anything according
to His will, He hears us.*

1 JOHN 5:14

THE GIFT OF JOY

But may the righteous be glad and rejoice
before God; may they be happy and joyful.

PSALM 68:3

Lord,

If I look at my painful circumstances and the evil in this world, it's hard to keep a smile on my face. I see suffering. Hatred. Loneliness and lies. Your people are persecuted and the innocent, oppressed. I struggle to see light in the darkness around me.

Yet I want to receive the happiness and joy You hold for those who love You. Show me how You use every difficulty for good in the end. Refresh my hope in Your promise to make all things new (Isaiah 43:19). Fill me with praise for the life and salvation I've found in Jesus.

Let me celebrate the heavenly treasures that are mine and be always captivated by Your love. Let my joy shine Your light to everyone.

Amen.

MORE OF YOU

My heart says of You, "Seek His face!"
Your face, Lord, I will seek.

PSALM 27:8

Lord,

My life is full of distractions. The voices of my family call for attention every hour of the day. A never-ending flow of emails and messages demands a response. The calendar and long to-do list remind me to stay on task each moment. Under the "tyranny of the urgent," I neglect to spend quiet time with You.

Draw me away from the busyness, Lord. I'm lonely for Your voice. My spirit grows dry and weary without the refreshment of Your Word. Detached from Your presence, I lose perspective and forget what's most important. My patience, clear thinking, and sense of peace begin to suffer.

Speak to me, Lord, as I seek Your face. Help me to abide in You. Become the constant focus of my days. Your love is everything.

Amen.

WILLING TO SUBMIT

Let everyone be subject to the governing authorities, for there is no authority except that which God has established.

ROMANS 13:1

Lord,

The failures of my government leaders grieve my heart. The innocent are denied justice. The wealthy are given an influential voice while the needy remain unheard. Denying their assignment to serve the public, leaders work and strive for their own gain. It's difficult to submit to government figures I don't trust or admire.

Your Word makes it plain – You want Your children to respect and obey those in authority. Help me to see Your hand of protection and care in the systems of leadership around me. Give me integrity to obey the law, pay what's due, and show respect.

Let Your wisdom guide my opinions and my votes. Show me how to conduct myself in my community so Your name is honored at all times.

Amen.

I BELIEVE

"Blessed is she who has believed that the Lord would fulfill His promises to her!"

Lord,

Your "very great and precious promises" (2 Peter 1:4) give me joy in life today and hope for the future to come. I know that every sin I confess to You will be forgiven.

You say I can face the road ahead with courage because You stay by my side. When the darkness is overwhelming, I remember Your plan to make all things new in the end. No matter how great my trouble or how intimidating my enemies might be, I am promised Your help, love, and peace beyond understanding.

Guard my heart from doubting Your Word. I want to take hold of every blessing found in trusting You. Write Your perfect truth on my heart and mind and help me to live by it, always (Hebrews 10:16).

Amen.

MY SOURCE
OF STRENGTH

*He gives strength to the weary and
increases the power of the weak.*

ISAIAH 40:29

Lord,

You called me to help and serve, encourage and love in Your name. Yet the needs around me feel overwhelming. I have so little to give. My knowledge and experience fall short of the wisdom required. The demands for my attention use up my energy and patience. I feel too weak and small to make a difference.

Fill me with Your strength, Lord. Make Your power perfect in my weakness (2 Corinthians 12:9). Out of Your heavenly wealth, provide resources I can share with those in need. Build my spiritual muscles so I don't "become weary in doing good" (Galatians 6:9).

Surround me with believers who will help me up when I'm falling down (Ecclesiastes 4:9-10). Help me to bear with others' limitations so I can love them like Jesus does.

Amen.

The earnest prayer of a righteous person has great power and produces wonderful results.

JAMES 5:16

GOD'S WONDERFUL WILL

*For everything in the world – the lust of the flesh,
the lust of the eyes, and the pride of life – comes
not from the Father but from the world.
The world and its desires pass away,
but whoever does the will of God lives forever.*

1 JOHN 2:16-17

Lord,

Desires wage war in my heart. I want more of You – Your truth, love, wisdom, and mercy. Yet the world wants to feed my pride and appetite for sin. I'm tempted to take my eyes off of You and chase after lesser things.

Be my greatest delight today. Let the hope of eternal treasure in heaven surpass any other craving. Keep me from striving after material things, entertainment, or status. Instead, move me to serve You and love others in Your name.

May I pursue our "good, pleasing, and perfect will" (Romans 12:2) as I walk in Your ways.

Amen.

FACING FORWARD

*"Forget the former things; do not dwell
on the past. See, I am doing a new thing!
Now it springs up; do you not perceive it?"*

Isaiah 43:18-19

Lord,

I wear shame like a tattoo on my chest. "For I know my transgressions, and my sin is always before me" (Psalm 51:3). I can't forget the past. The enemy whispers in my ear that I'm a failure. I'll never change. I'm not worthy to be called Your daughter. I struggle to believe You're making me new.

Help me to trust Your Word. Through Jesus, I'm forgiven. My sin-debt is paid in full. I'm chosen and cherished. My name is written on Your hands (Isaiah 49:16), and nothing can separate me from Your love (Romans 8:39). No one can accuse me – I am innocent and free.

Forgive my doubt and help my unbelief. Let me celebrate my new life in You!

Amen.

THE MIND OF CHRIST

*We take captive every thought to make
it obedient to Christ.*

2 CORINTHIANS 10:5

Lord,

My thoughts have a life of their own. I imagine rude, clever comebacks when I'm offended to take my opponent down.

Jealousy dominates my mind when I see a friend's beauty, her success, or her possessions. A mental list of worries and complaints runs through every waking moment. It's difficult to put a halt to my wrong thinking and meditate on Your truth.

Teach me how to take control of my mind. Help me to dwell on Your works and Your Word all the time (Psalm 143:5).

Keep me sensitive to the Spirit's correction. Spark creative ideas to serve and care for others. Give discernment to wisely choose what I read and view. When I'm negative, remind me of Your love. Continue to make me new and give me the mind of Christ.

Amen.

PATIENCE AND PEACE

*Everyone should be quick to listen, slow
to speak and slow to become angry, because
human anger does not produce the
righteousness that God desires.*

JAMES 1:19-20

Lord,

Daily interruptions sabotage my organized plans. Others' mistakes interfere with achieving my goals. No matter how much time, attention, and help I give my loved ones, they still complain and fail to do what's right. When I struggle, I feel overlooked and alone. Anger builds in my heart until it spills out in harsh and ugly ways.

I want to be patient like You, Lord. You listen to every prayer and respond with love. When I'm selfish and sinful, You forgive and show compassion (Psalm 103:13). Quiet my temper so I respond to others with gentle kindness.

Help me to listen well before I speak. Give me a merciful spirit so I live and love as a peacemaker.

Amen.

NEVER FORGET

*I will remember the deeds of the LORD; yes,
I will remember Your miracles of long ago.
I will consider all Your works and meditate
on all Your mighty deeds.*

PSALM 77:11-12

Lord,

I remember how You met my needs and rescued me from trouble. In times of confusion, You marked a clear path for my feet. Answered prayers put down deep roots of faith in my heart.

Nights of weeping gave way to joyful mornings, just as You promised (Psalm 30:5). Over and over, You proved Your power and love in my life.

I'm walking through another dark valley today. Blessings were snatched from my hands. Doors have closed in my face. Yet no matter my losses, I still have You. Your love is constant. You remain by my side. Help me to remember Your works in the past so I hold on to hope for tomorrow.

Amen.

COURAGEOUS PRAYERS

Do not be anxious about anything, but in every situation, by prayer and petition, with thanksgiving, present your requests to God.

PHILIPPIANS 4:6

Lord,

My mind is flooded with worries today. What if I fail to accomplish what's expected of me? What if this separation from my loved one never ends? What if the money runs out just when it's needed most? In the night, anxiety steals my sleep. When daylight comes, I'm weary, distracted, and afraid.

Forgive me for my foolish doubts. Your love never failed in the past and the future is held securely in Your hands. Your Word makes it plain: "[I] do not have because [I] do not ask" (James 4:2).

Teach me to pray at all times. Fill me with gratitude for each day's mercy and kindness. Let my heart be pure in all I ask as I rely on You for everything.

Amen.

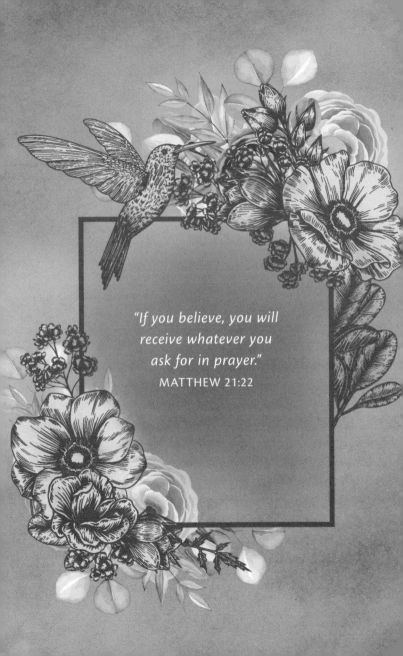

"If you believe, you will receive whatever you ask for in prayer."

MATTHEW 21:22

Joanna Teigen and her husband, Rob, have been married for over 25 years and are loving life with two sons, three daughters, and a beautiful daughter-in-law. As the founders of their ministry, Growing Home Together, they believe their vows are for always, children are a gift, and prayer is powerful. The Teigens currently live in West Michigan and are passionate to help people experience the power of God in their families.

The couple have authored several books including *Mr & Mrs: 366 Devotions for Couples, 101 Prayers for My Daughter* and *101 Prayers for My Son*.